PERSPECTIVES ON AMERICAN PROGRESS

THE INTERNET
CONNECTS US ALL

BY DUCHESS HARRIS, JD, PHD
WITH HEATHER C. HUDAK

Cover image: Computer scientist Leonard Kleinrock points to the computer that made the first connection to another computer.

Core Library
An Imprint of Abdo Publishing
abdopublishing.com

abdopublishing.com

Published by Abdo Publishing, a division of ABDO, PO Box 398166, Minneapolis, Minnesota 55439. Copyright © 2019 by Abdo Consulting Group, Inc. International copyrights reserved in all countries. No part of this book may be reproduced in any form without written permission from the publisher. Core Library™ is a trademark and logo of Abdo Publishing.

Printed in the United States of America, North Mankato, Minnesota
042018
092018

THIS BOOK CONTAINS RECYCLED MATERIALS

Cover Photo: Reed Saxon/AP Images
Interior Photos: Reed Saxon/AP Images, 1; Praetorian Photo/iStockphoto, 4–5; Red Line Editorial, 6; Detlev van Ravenswaay/Science Source, 10–11; Fred Prouser/Reuters/Newscom, 17; Douglas A. Sonders/US PGA Tour/Getty Images, 20–21; Tim Wagner/ZumaPress/Newscom, 24; Martial Trezzini/Keystone/AP Images, 26–27, 43; Shutterstock Images, 31; Uber Images/Shutterstock Images, 34–35; Ni Yanqiang/Imaginechina/AP Images, 39; StockVector/Shutterstock Images, 40

Editor: Marie Pearson
Imprint Designer: Maggie Villaume
Series Design Direction: Ryan Gale

Library of Congress Control Number: 2017962651

Publisher's Cataloging-in-Publication Data

Names: Harris, Duchess, author. | Hudak, Heather C., author.
Title: The internet connects us all / by Duchess Harris and Heather C. Hudak.
Description: Minneapolis, Minnesota : Abdo Publishing, 2019. | Series: Perspectives on American progress | Includes online resources and index.
Identifiers: ISBN 9781532114915 (lib.bdg.) | ISBN 9781532154744 (ebook)
Subjects: LCSH: Internet--History--Juvenile literature. | World Wide Web--Juvenile literature. | Internet browsers (Computer programs)--Juvenile literature.
Classification: DDC 004.678--dc23

CONTENTS

CHAPTER ONE
Bringing the World Together 4

CHAPTER TWO
Introducing ARPANET 10

CHAPTER THREE
A New Protocol 20

CHAPTER FOUR
Creating the Web 26

CHAPTER FIVE
Internet Ownership 34

Important Dates. 42

Stop and Think 44

Glossary 45

Online Resources 46

Learn More 46

About the Authors 47

Index 48

CHAPTER ONE

BRINGING THE WORLD TOGETHER

Have you ever used Skype to talk to someone on the other side of the world? Maybe you have searched Google for sources to write a school report. The internet connects us to people and information from all over the world.

It is hard to picture a world without Google or Instagram. But the internet is a fairly new invention. In fact, it was only made widely available in the early 1990s. Before then, the only way to share information was through books, computer disks, and other forms of hard copy. If you wanted to send a note to a friend,

The internet gives people in many locations access to information from around the world.

INTERNET USERS AROUND THE WORLD

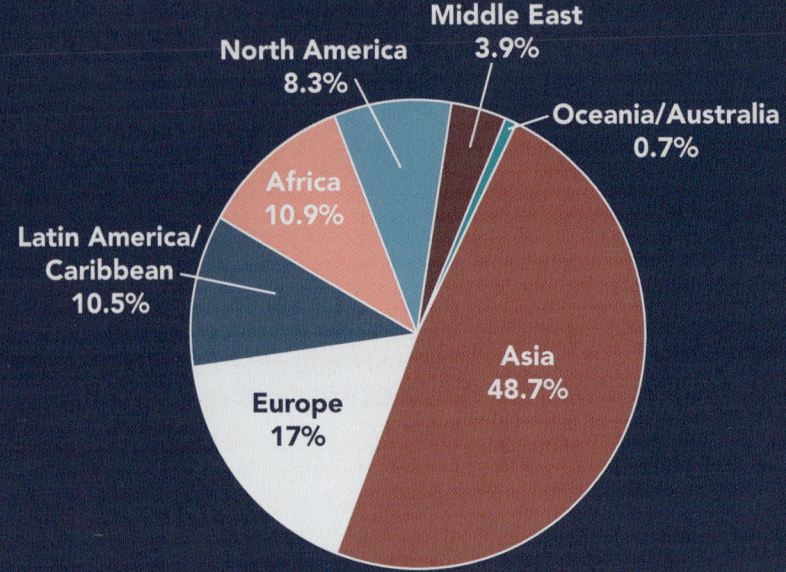

This chart shows what percentage of total internet users came from each region in March 2018. Why do you think some regions made up a greater percentage of internet users than others?

you had to write it on a piece of paper. It could take days to arrive in the mail.

Thanks to the internet, the world is at our fingertips. We can use web pages to teach each other about new topics. We can use social media to share pictures of our lives in real-time. We can even watch videos on demand.

Understanding the Internet

The internet is a huge collection of computers. They are connected by wires, cables, radio waves, and satellite links. They form a network. The internet is used to move data from one computer to another. Data might include web pages, files, music, and emails. One way to think of the internet is to compare it to a system of highways. A computer network is made up of many roads linked together. Data is like the cars. It uses highways to move from one place to another.

The internet is made up of hundreds of millions of computers around the world. Some store large amounts of data. They pass the data on as needed. These computers are called servers. There are different kinds of servers. File servers store documents. Mail servers store messages. Web servers store web pages. A computer that pulls data off of the internet is called a client. There are many more clients than servers. A router is a type of computer that connects other computers to the internet.

The World Wide Web

The internet and the World Wide Web, called the Web, are closely related. But they are actually two different things. The Web is an application that runs on the internet. It is the collection of public web pages found online. Web pages are made of text, images, and hyperlinks. A collection of web pages that are linked together on the same server is called a website. The Web is the most common way for people to access data on the internet. Web pages are written in computer code. Browsers such as Internet Explorer and Google Chrome translate the code

SCREEN TIME

There are nearly 4 billion people on the internet around the world. Approximately 87 percent of Americans use the internet. Each day, US adults spend nearly 11 hours looking at a screen. Facebook is the top social media site with nearly 2 billion users. Most users spend approximately 50 minutes on it each day. Some doctors are worried so much screen time can lead to obesity, poor sleep, and poor performance in school.

into text and graphics. People use browsers to view web pages. Users can visit different websites with a browser like they can watch different channels on a television.

Many scientists, engineers, and researchers built the internet as we know it today. Thanks to them, the world's information is just a few clicks away for many people. This invention changed the world.

PERSPECTIVES

AMERICANS WITHOUT INTERNET

Thirteen percent of Americans are not online. Of these, approximately one-third say they have no interest in the internet at all. Another one-third find the internet hard to use. Some think they are too old to learn a new technology. One-fifth cannot afford a computer or internet fees. Black and Hispanic people are more likely than white people to rely on free, public internet access. Those with low incomes or less education are also less likely to have internet access. The rest have several other reasons they do not use the internet.

CHAPTER
TWO

INTRODUCING ARPANET

The late 1940s was a time of tension between the United States and the Soviet Union. This time was known as the Cold War. The war was not fought using weapons. Instead, the two countries competed in science and technology. Each tried to build bigger bombs or send people into space. But there was a fear the war could turn into a real battle.

By the 1960s, both countries had nuclear weapons. There were Soviet and US satellites in space. The US Department of Defense (DOD) Advanced Research Projects Agency (ARPA) wanted to build a computer system that

The Soviet Union put the first satellite, Sputnik, into space in 1957.

> ## PERSPECTIVES
> ### COMMUNIST FEARS AND THE COLD WAR
> The United States and the Soviet Union had very different political systems. The United States was capitalist. It gave people the freedom to own property and build their wealth. The Soviets were Communist. All property and wealth was controlled by the government. Some Americans thought Communism was good. But many others did not want it to come to the United States. They feared the Soviets would try to spread Communism to other countries.

could not be destroyed by a Soviet attack. It would be made of many computers in different places. They would be linked through a network.

Connecting Computers

Joseph Carl Robnett Licklider believed people could use computers to help them think and make decisions. In 1962 Licklider wrote about his vision for a computer network. People all over the world could use it to get data from other parts of the world. ARPA hired him to lead a project that would make his vision come true. They wanted him to build a computer network for the military.

Licklider began to share his ideas with others at ARPA. He wrote about the benefits of a global computer network. He talked about connecting computers so that researchers could easily share information. He talked about the potential for online banking and other features of the modern internet. His excitement spread. People wanted to help Licklider achieve his vision.

Licklider never actually built ARPA's network himself. He left ARPA in 1964 to work for IBM. But his ideas had a big impact on his peers. They paved the way for the world's first computer network, ARPANET.

Digital Data

In 1964 electrical engineer Paul Baran came up with an idea called packet switching. It was a way to link computers. Packet switching used digital systems.

ELIZABETH FEINLER

Elizabeth Feinler is an information and computer scientist. She played a key role in ARPANET's success. In 1972 she started writing a guide to help organize ARPANET. There was no easy way to search for data on ARPANET. Feinler's guide was similar to a phone book. It listed all the people on ARPANET and their locations. She had hundreds of pages of documents that helped people use ARPANET. Later she came up with the .com domain name structure. It was used to describe companies that sold products and services through the internet. She also came up with the idea for other domain name structures, such as .org, .edu, and .gov.

It only sent data as needed in small amounts. Each piece of data was broken into smaller packets. Each one was an equal size. The packets were sent through the network one by one. They could be sent out of order. They could even travel different routes. Then they were put back together when they reached their destination. A large piece of data might be made of thousands of packets. ARPA used packet switching as the basis for ARPANET.

With packet switching, many different computers were linked together using the same cables. Each one was permanently connected to the network. The link between computers never stopped sending data.

Building a Network

In 1966 ARPA hired Robert Taylor to lead the development of a computer network program. ARPA was funding three different computer research projects. Each one was at a different university. Taylor had to use a different computer to connect to each project. He did not like having three computers on his desk at work. His frustration led to a new idea. Taylor wanted just one computer to access all information. Taylor pitched his idea to ARPA. They gave him $1 million for the project. It was the start of ARPANET.

Taylor had some of the best people in the world working for him. One of these people was computer scientist Leonard Kleinrock. He was working on his idea for packet switching at approximately the same time Baran came up with his ideas. Kleinrock was excited to test packet switching. He and a team at the University of California, Los Angeles (UCLA) wrote the communication protocol for ARPANET in the 1960s. It was called Network Control Program (NCP). A protocol is a set of rules computers use to exchange data over a network. Computers need a common protocol to be able to speak to each other. NCP was based on packet switching.

On October 29, 1969, Kleinrock's team sent the world's first packet-switched message between two computers. UCLA student Charley Kline connected with a computer at the Stanford Research Institute. Kline had been working on the ARPANET project for some time. One day, he decided to test it. It was 10:30 p.m. when Kline sent the message to Bill Duvall at Stanford

UCLA kept the computer that Kline used in a storage closet for more than 20 years before putting it on display.

Research Institute. It was two letters: L and O. He meant to send the word *login*, but the computer crashed. Later that night, he sent the whole word. Kline jotted down a few notes about the event and went to bed. Duvall grabbed a burger and went home. There was no big celebration or news release. But it had a huge impact on the world.

ARPANET was finally real. At first it could perform only three tasks. It could log into a remote computer. It could print to a remote printer. It could send files between computers. Universities and research centers such as NASA soon started joining the ARPANET network. Over the next ten years, many scientists came up with innovations to improve ARPANET.

STRAIGHT TO THE SOURCE

In 1960 Licklider called for a symbiosis between humans and computers. This meant humans and computers would work closely together to perform tasks. He believed this would help them perform tasks.

The purposes of this paper are to present the concept and, hopefully, to foster the development of man-computer symbiosis by analyzing some problems . . . and pointing out a few questions to which research answers are needed. The hope is that, in not too many years, human brains and computing machines will be coupled together very tightly, and that the resulting partnership will think as no human brain has ever thought and process data in a way not approached by the information-handling machines we know today.

Source: J. C. R. Licklider. "Man-Computer Symbiosis." *IRE Transactions on Human Factors in Electronics* 1 (March 1960): 4–11. *MIT Computer Science & Artificial Intelligence Lab*. Web. Accessed December 21, 2017.

What's the Big Idea?

Take a close look at this passage. What is the main point Licklider is trying to make about how humans and computers can work together? Why was it important that humans and computers work well together?

CHAPTER
THREE

A NEW PROTOCOL

Vinton Cerf and Robert Kahn first met while working on ARPANET. Cerf, a graduate student, helped write the NCP. Kahn was an electrical engineer at a company called Bolt Beranek & Newman. The company helped build the ARPANET system. Kahn wanted Cerf to do a series of tests on ARPANET. The two men worked closely together. Kahn would come up with a set of requirements for ARPANET. Then Cerf would write them overnight.

By 1973 Kahn decided he wanted to build a network of packet-switching networks.

Vinton Cerf, *left***, and Robert Kahn,** *right foreground***, each received a Presidential Medal of Freedom for their work in developing the internet.**

Any computer or network would be able to talk to any other computer or network. They did not even need to use the same types of hardware or software. Kahn wondered how to bring his idea to life. He turned to his friend, Cerf, to help him find a solution.

PERSPECTIVES
SOVIET COMPUTER CONNECTIONS

Ukrainian mathematician Viktor Glushkov worked in the Soviet Union. He came up with many ideas for connecting computers across networks. One of them was called the All-State Automated System. Much like ARPANET, it would connect computers across a network. By 1970 it was ready to be put into place. But Glushkov did not receive the support and funds he needed from the government to make it happen.

Perfect Partners

In the spring of 1973, Kahn went to see Cerf at Stanford University. It only took one meeting for Kahn and Cerf to come up with a plan. They traveled back and forth a few times to talk about the project. That summer, they wrote a paper about their idea. It laid the foundation for a new protocol called

Transmission Control Protocol (TCP). They knew they were on the verge of something great.

Cerf joined the ARPA team in 1976. He and Kahn worked on the TCP. By 1977 the system had become a set of protocols called Transmission Control Protocol/Internet Protocol (TCP/IP). TCP was used to break up data into segments. It put them back together when they reached their destination. IP was used to transmit the segments across the network.

Standard System

In 1980 the DOD made plans to upgrade its hardware. In 1982 ARPANET started using TCP/IP. It quickly became the standard for all sites. Not everyone was happy about it. Some people

JUDITH ESTRIN

Judith Estrin was studying computer science at Stanford when Cerf began working on the idea for TCP/IP. She was part of the team that built the protocol. Estrin is now seen as one of the pioneers of the internet. She has cofounded eight technology companies since 1981.

Cerf speaks around the world about internet use and issues.

wanted to keep NCP. But ARPANET's technology was changing on January 1, 1983, whether people liked it or not. Cerf did a test of the new system for a full day. He wanted to make sure it worked. He turned off all NCP sites. Only TCP/IP sites could work. That fall, he did another test. This time, he turned off NCP sites for two days.

When the New Year came, all NCP sites were shut down. The next year, the DOD made TCP/IP the standard for all military networks. TCP/IP laid the groundwork for the modern-day internet. To date, TCP/IP is the standard for all networks around the world.

Cerf and Kahn became known as the fathers of the internet. TCP/IP made it possible for anyone to build a piece of the internet. They could connect to it from anywhere in the world. They just had to use the standard protocol. Cerf and Kahn knew their idea would open up a whole new world. But they had no idea just how big it would become. Both continued working on the internet into the 2010s. They have won many awards for their work.

FURTHER EVIDENCE

Chapter Three has quite a bit of information about the achievements of Vinton Cerf and Robert Kahn. What is the main point of this chapter? What key evidence supports this point? Go to the article about Cerf and Kahn at the website below. Find a quote from the website that supports the chapter's main point.

DR. VINTON CERF AND DR. ROBERT KAHN: MEDAL OF FREEDOM RECIPIENTS
abdocorelibrary.com/internet-connects-us-all

CHAPTER
FOUR

CREATING THE WEB

By the late 1980s, millions of computers had been linked as part of the internet. Scientists and researchers used it to send messages and data around the world. British computer scientist Tim Berners-Lee thought the internet had lots of potential. He wanted to make it easier for people to access the internet.

Berners-Lee worked at the European Organization for Nuclear Research (CERN) in Geneva, Switzerland. He was tired of how much time it took to share data with his peers. Each researcher stored project details on a different computer. Whenever he wanted to

Tim Berners-Lee stands with the very first Web server.

know the details of a certain project, he had to log on to the appropriate computer. It was often easier to simply talk about a project over a cup of coffee or send an email about it.

Berners-Lee was sure he could find a better way to do business. CERN scientists worked all over the world. What if they could use the internet to share ideas? They could place their data online. Others could access it anytime. There was no need to email the data back and forth. If a scientist noted another person's work in their research, they could link right to that work. Berners-Lee began mapping out an idea to use the internet to connect people.

A Fresh Idea

In March 1989, Berners-Lee wrote a paper. In it, he talked about how the internet could connect the thousands of people working at CERN. He wanted to create a web of information. It would be linked together using hypertext. People would use buttons on a screen to jump from one piece of information to another.

Berners-Lee gave the paper to his boss, Mike Sendall. Sendall thought it was an interesting idea. He gave Berners-Lee some time to work on it in September 1990. By October, Berners-Lee had written the basic software he needed for his project. The software had several parts.

Hypertext Markup Language (HTML) is a series of symbols and codes. It is used to create documents called web pages.

PERSPECTIVES
MIKE SENDALL

If it were not for Mike Sendall, there may never have been a Web. Sendall was Berners-Lee's boss at CERN. He thought the project was a good idea. But it was not the kind of work CERN did. Still, Sendall said he would not tell anyone if Berners-Lee spent some time writing the software for the Web. Berners-Lee likely would not have been given the time if he had to put in an official request with CERN.

HTML includes instructions that tell a computer how text and images should look on a computer screen.

Berners-Lee also wrote the world's first web browser. A browser turned the HTML code into a format that showed on a computer screen. The most common web browsers today are Internet Explorer, Google Chrome, Mozilla Firefox, and Safari.

The Uniform Resource Identifier (URI) is used to name pages on the internet. It is a type of address that shows where a web page is located. It is made up of letters, numbers, and symbols. Each web page has its own URI.

Hypertext Transfer Protocol (HTTP) lets computers talk to one another and transfer data. It is used to send and receive web pages and files on the internet. When a person enters a website address in a browser, the browser sends an HTTP request to the web server.

People who build websites need to know HTML.

```html
TYPE html>
 xmlns="http://www.w3.org/199
>
title>Sample HTML Page</title
    <meta http-equiv="Content-
    <meta property="og:type"  c
    <meta property="og:url"  co
    <meta name="robots"  conten
    <meta name="author"  conten
    <link href="http://www.som
    <link href="http://www.som
    <script type='text/javascr
    <script type='text/javascr
d>
>
class="mainHeader">
div class='logo'></div>
```

> ### WORLD WIDE WEB FOUNDATION
> Berners-Lee cofounded the World Wide Web Foundation with his future wife, Rosemary Leith, in 2009. The World Wide Web Foundation believes everyone in the world should have access to the Web. It aims to ensure all people can use the Web for free in order to better their lives.

HTTP tells the server to transmit the web page the person asks to see.

World Wide Web

Before the end of 1990, Berners-Lee posted the first web page on the internet. He took every chance he could to talk about his invention. Within a year, a few people outside of CERN were given access to the system Berners-Lee had built. In April 1993, Berners-Lee made the software available to the public for free. Now anyone could use it to make web pages. It sparked an internet frenzy that has not stopped.

When Berners-Lee invented the Web, he knew it had the power to do both good and bad. People all over the world could share news, views, and information. However, they could also use the Web to spread false information. Over the years, Berners-Lee has become concerned about some of the content available on the Web. He works with governments and organizations to find ways to make the Web a safe and positive place.

EXPLORE ONLINE

Chapter Four talks about how Tim Berners-Lee invented the Web. Visit the website below. It has more information on this topic. Does the site answer any of the questions you had about Berners-Lee's work and the Web?

SIR TIM BERNERS-LEE
abdocorelibrary.com/internet-connects-us-all

CHAPTER
FIVE

INTERNET OWNERSHIP

The internet was built in the United States. But it belongs to everyone in the world. Anyone can add to it and build new technologies for it. The internet is made of many networks all over the world. There is no one person, government, or organization that owns these networks.

Similarly, the internet is free and open to use. Net neutrality makes companies and governments treat internet data equally. Without it, an internet provider could block or slow down certain web pages.

Anyone with access to the internet can create blogs or social media accounts or add comments to what others share.

PERSPECTIVES
NET NEUTRALITY

When people log onto the internet, they want to view any web page they choose. This is net neutrality. People decide what they want to see on the Web. Service providers do not decide for them. All sites are treated equally. Companies cannot pay a service provider more money to make sure their website works better or faster. Service providers cannot block sites. Some people do not like net neutrality. They believe service providers should have control over what people see on the Web. They think it will drive innovation and competition between companies. In 2018 the US government was debating net neutrality laws.

Around the World

The internet has grown over the decades. In 1996 there were only approximately 40 million people online. In 2018 there were more than 4 billion internet users around the world. Still, more than one-half of people do not have internet access.

In many parts of the world, the internet has had a major impact on the way people live and work. Businesses use the internet to share information and perform daily tasks. Social networks are the most common ways for people to communicate. Developing and emerging nations are not as well connected as wealthier countries. In Pakistan only 8 percent of people have internet access. However, these nations still see the internet as a powerful tool for education, business, and communication. As they continue to grow and develop, the internet will play a big role in people's lives. Because of the internet's growth, groups have formed to make sure it continues to work around the world.

Governance Groups

Many groups set standards for how the internet works, grows, and runs. Some members are experts on technology. Others understand policies and laws. Some work for universities or governments. Each one of these people wants to see the internet grow for years to come. They look for the best ways to make this happen.

One important group is the Internet Corporation for Assigned Names and Numbers (ICANN). It makes sure that no two computers in the world have the same address. It assigns a unique name and number to each computer. This makes it possible to send data from one specific computer to another.

CONTROL OVER ICANN

ICANN started in 1998. It was run by the US Department of Commerce. The United Nations and other global organizations did not like that it was under the control of one country. They thought there should be more involvement from groups around the world. In 2009 the United States gave up its rights to control ICANN. It took one seat on the board. Representatives from 11 other countries filled the remaining seats.

The Internet Architecture Board oversees the technology used to develop the internet. It comes up with technical standards for all people to use. This ensures as many people as possible around the world can connect to the internet. And each year, members of

ICANN's president and CEO from 2012 to 2016 was Fadi Chehadé.

the Internet Governance Forum meet to talk about how policies can make the internet better. They look for ways to solve problems such as security threats.

Beyond Desktops

Gone are the days of needing a phone line to connect to the internet. In a wireless world, more and more people are able to get online. Today, the internet connects much more than just computer networks.

INTERNET OF THINGS

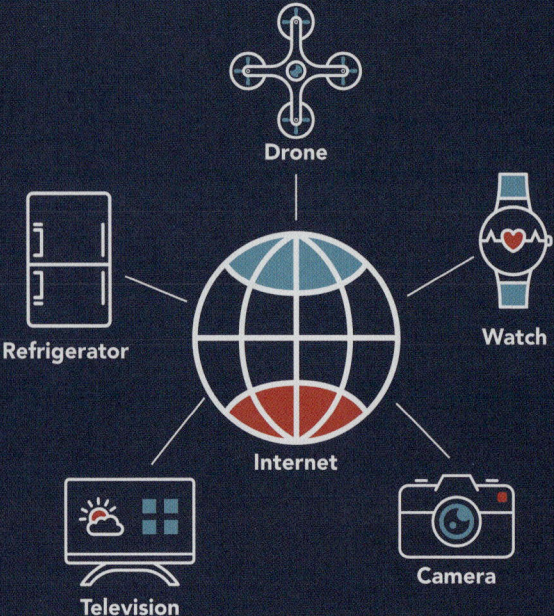

The Internet of Things is making the world smart. From just one device such as a smartphone, people can control many things through the internet. It can make life easier. But some people worry that the Internet of Things is not secure. People can hack devices. They cause a nuisance or listen to conversations. Do you have any items from the image above that can be controlled through the internet? Can you think of any others?

Mobile devices including tablets and smartphones use the internet. Other devices are being connected to the internet, too. The Internet of Things includes cars, appliances, and objects that use the internet to run certain features. It is just another example of how the internet connects us all.

STRAIGHT TO THE SOURCE

In 2013 leaders from some of the most important internet governance groups met to talk about the future of the internet. On October 7, they wrote about the results of their meeting:

> The Internet and World Wide Web have brought major benefits in social and economic development worldwide. Both have been built and governed in the public interest through unique mechanisms for global multistakeholder Internet cooperation, which have been intrinsic to their success. The leaders discussed the clear need to continually strengthen and evolve these mechanisms, in truly substantial ways, to be able to address emerging issues faced by stakeholders in the Internet.
>
> Source: "Montevideo Statement on the Future of Internet Cooperation." *ICAAN*. ICANN, October 7, 2013. Web. Accessed December 9, 2017.

Changing Minds

This passage discusses the importance of global Internet cooperation. Take a position on this cooperation, then imagine that your best friend has the opposite opinion. Write a short essay trying to change your friend's mind. Make sure you detail your opinion and your reasons for it. Include facts that support your reasons.

IMPORTANT DATES

1962
Joseph Carl Robnett Licklider writes about his vision for a computer network. ARPA hires him to work on his idea.

1964
Electrical engineer Paul Baran comes up with the idea for packet switching.

1966
ARPA hires Robert Taylor to lead the development of a computer network program. He asks Leonard Kleinrock to help him build ARPANET.

1969
Kleinrock's team at UCLA sends the world's first packet-switched message between two computers on October 29.

1982
TCP/IP becomes the standard for all sites.

1983
All NCP sites are shut down on January 1. The US Department of Defense makes TCP/IP the standard for all military networks the next year.

1989
In March, Tim Berners-Lee comes up with an idea to use the internet to connect thousands of CERN employees.

1990
Berners-Lee invents the Web in October.

1993
In April, Berners-Lee makes the source code to his software free to the public.

STOP AND
THINK

Surprise Me

Chapter One discusses ARPANET and the history of the internet. After reading this book, what two or three facts about the internet did you find most surprising? Write a few sentences about each fact. Why did you find each fact surprising?

Tell the Tale

Chapter Four of this book discusses how Tim Berners-Lee came up with the idea for the Web. Imagine you have come up with a new computer program to help people share ideas. Write 200 words about the software you would build. What would it do?

Dig Deeper

After reading this book, what questions do you still have about the internet? With an adult's help, find a few reliable sources that can help you answer your questions. Write a paragraph about what you learned.

GLOSSARY

application
a computer software program that performs a specific function

digital
computer data written as a series of 0s and 1s

domain name
a company, organization, or other group's name on the internet not used by anyone else

hardware
the physical parts of a computer and its systems, such as wires, screens, and keyboards

hyperlinks
clickable links from one file or document to another

network
a group of connected people or objects

policy
a standard way of doing things that is used by groups and organizations

protocol
the set rules for sending data between two devices

software
programs and information used to run a computer

standard
an accepted normal way of doing something

ONLINE RESOURCES

To learn more about the development of the internet, visit our free resource websites below.

Visit **abdocorelibrary.com** for free Common Core resources for teachers and students, including vetted activities, multimedia, and booklinks, for deeper subject comprehension.

Visit **abdobooklinks.com** for free additional online weblinks for further learning. These links are routinely monitored and updated to provide the most current information available.

LEARN MORE

Gagne, Tammy. *Women in Computer Science*. Minneapolis, MN: Abdo, 2017.

Harris, Duchess, and Elisabeth Herschbach. *Your Personalized Internet*. Minneapolis, MN: Abdo, 2018.

ABOUT THE AUTHORS

Duchess Harris, JD, PhD
Professor Harris is the chair of the American Studies department at Macalester College and curator of the Duchess Harris Collection of ABDO books. She is the author and coauthor of recently released ABDO books including *Hidden Human Computers: The Black Women of NASA*, *Black Lives Matter*, and *Race and Policing*. Before working with ABDO, she authored several other books on the topics of race, culture, and American history. She served as an associate editor for *Litigation News*, the American Bar Association Section of Litigation's quarterly flagship publication, and was the first editor in chief of *Law Raza*, an interactive online journal covering race and the law, published at William Mitchell College of Law. She has earned a PhD in American Studies from the University of Minnesota and a JD from William Mitchell College of Law.

Heather C. Hudak
Heather C. Hudak has written hundreds of books for children and edited thousands more. She loves learning about new topics, traveling the world, and spending time with her husband and many pets.

INDEX

Advanced Research Projects Agency (ARPA), 11–15, 23
ARPANET, 13–18, 21, 22, 23–24

Baran, Paul, 13, 16
Berners-Lee, Tim, 27–33

Cerf, Vinton, 21–25
Cold War, 11, 12

Department of Defense (DOD), US, 11, 23, 24
Duvall, Bill, 16–18

Estrin, Judith, 23
European Organization for Nuclear Research (CERN), 27–28, 29, 32

Feinler, Elizabeth, 14

Glushkov, Viktor, 22
Google, 5, 8, 30

Hypertext Markup Language (HTML), 29–30
Hypertext Transfer Protocol (HTTP), 30–31

Internet Architecture Board, 38
Internet Corporation for Assigned Names and Numbers (ICANN), 38
Internet Governance Form, 39
Internet of Things, 40

Kahn, Robert, 21–23, 25
Kleinrock, Leonard, 16
Kline, Charley, 16–18

Leith, Rosemary, 32
Licklider, Joseph Carl Robnett, 12–13, 19

NASA, 18
net neutrality, 35, 36
Network Control Program (NCP), 16, 21, 24

Sendall, Mike, 29
Soviet Union, 11, 12, 22
Stanford Research Institute, 16

Taylor, Robert, 15
Transmission Control protocol/Internet Protocol (TCP/IP), 23–25

Uniform Resource Identifier (URI), 30
United Nations, 38
University of California, Los Angeles (UCLA), 16

World Wide Web (Web), 8, 29, 32–33, 36, 41